BAJC
10/19

INSIDE THE
NFL

KANSAS CITY
CHIEFS

BY TONY HUNTER

SportsZone

An Imprint of Abdo Publishing
abdobooks.com

abdobooks.com

Published by Abdo Publishing, a division of ABDO, PO Box 398166, Minneapolis, Minnesota 55439. Copyright © 2020 by Abdo Consulting Group, Inc. International copyrights reserved in all countries. No part of this book may be reproduced in any form without written permission from the publisher. SportsZone™ is a trademark and logo of Abdo Publishing.

Printed in the United States of America, North Mankato, Minnesota
032019
092019

THIS BOOK CONTAINS
RECYCLED MATERIALS

Cover Photo: Rick Wilson/AP Images
Interior Photos: NFL Photos/AP Images, 5, 12, 19, 27, 29; AP Images, 7, 9; Vernon Biever/AP Images, 11; Carl Linde/AP Images, 16; Rich Clarkson/Rich Clarkson Associates/AP Images, 24; Focus on Sport/Getty Images North America/Getty Images, 23, 43; David Stluka/AP Images, 32; Denis Poroy/AP Images, 35; G. Newman Lowrance/AP Images, 37, 41; Ed Zurga/AP Images, 38

Editor: Patrick Donnelly
Series Designer: Craig Hinton

Library of Congress Control Number: 2018965343

Publisher's Cataloging-in-Publication Data

Names: Hunter, Tony, author.
Title: Kansas City Chiefs / by Tony Hunter.
Description: Minneapolis, Minnesota : Abdo Publishing, 2020 | Series: Inside the NFL | Includes online resources and index.
Identifiers: ISBN 9781532118517 (lib. bdg.) | ISBN 9781532172694 (ebook)| ISBN 9781644941089 (pbk.)
Subjects: LCSH: Kansas City Chiefs (Football team)--Juvenile literature. | National Football League--Juvenile literature. | Football teams--Juvenile literature. | American football--Juvenile literature.
Classification: DDC 796.33264--dc23

TABLE OF
CONTENTS

CHAPTER 1

A NEW BEGINNING

The atmosphere was tense. The Kansas City Chiefs and the Green Bay Packers met at the Los Angeles Memorial Coliseum on January 15, 1967. The Chiefs were the American Football League (AFL) champions. The Packers had won the National Football League (NFL) championship.

This was the first AFL-NFL World Championship Game. It would later become known as Super Bowl I.

Each team was playing for the pride of its league. The NFL and AFL had agreed one year earlier to pit their champions against each other at the end of the season. Each league wanted to show that it was the stronger one. Given that the AFL had only been around for seven years, most people thought the more established NFL was the superior league.

Quarterback Len Dawson led the AFL champion Chiefs to Super Bowl I in January 1967.

SUPER BOWL I

The first Super Bowl was much different from what we are used to today. In fact, it was not even called the Super Bowl at the time. It was known as the AFL-NFL World Championship Game. It would be renamed Super Bowl I at a later date.

The contrasts started with the coin toss. Instead of inviting a former player or a celebrity to toss the coin, the game officials handled the duties. The halftime show didn't feature a pop diva or well-known rock band either. Instead, the marching bands from the University of Arizona and University of Michigan performed.

The fan experience was much different as well. The stadium was not even sold out. Tickets for the most expensive seat cost $12. Today a fan looking to attend the NFL's biggest game has to be willing to drop at least $1,000 for a ticket. Some ticket brokers charge thousands of dollars for the best seats at the game.

The Chiefs fought hard to change that perception. They set out to slow the Packers' famed running attack. In the process, they also were making legendary quarterback Bart Starr look simply ordinary.

Green Bay had opened the scoring with a touchdown pass from Starr to Max McGee. But Kansas City soon answered. In the second quarter, Chiefs quarterback Len Dawson marched his team down the field. On the sixth play of the drive, Dawson was forced to scramble. But he connected with fullback Curtis McClinton for a 7-yard touchdown pass.

✕ Kansas City running back Mike Garrett carries the ball against the Green Bay Packers in Super Bowl I.

At halftime the Packers' lead was only 14–10. The Chiefs and their coach, Hank Stram, could sense an upset. So could the 63,036 fans in attendance. But it was not to be.

The Chiefs' momentum faded early in the second half. Dawson moved the Chiefs to their own 49-yard line. But on the next play, the Packers blitzed, and Dawson struggled under the pressure. He tried to throw downfield, but his pass was tipped. The ball wobbled through the air before landing in the hands of Packers defensive back Willie Wood, who returned it all the way to the Chiefs' 5-yard line. The Packers scored a touchdown on the next play.

Green Bay never looked back. The Packers scored 21 unanswered points in a 35–10 win over the Chiefs.

Kansas City defensive tackle Jerry Mays was quick to credit the Packers for their victory. But he did not think the Chiefs were as bad as the final score indicated.

"We had to stop Green Bay on those third-and-one and -two plays," Mays said. "Then they killed us on third-and-six and third-and-long. The way I see it, we lost our poise after Wood's interception. The Packers themselves beat us in the first half, then the Packers and the Packer myth beat us in the second."

Chiefs defensive tackle Buck Buchanan did not believe the Chiefs were that much worse than the Packers, either. He was eager for a rematch as soon as the final whistle blew.

"I'd like to play them again next year, or next week, or even tomorrow," Buchanan said.

Kansas City didn't get another shot at the Packers. However, they did get one more chance to represent the AFL in the Super Bowl.

Chiefs coach Hank Stram is carried away in celebration after his team defeated the Minnesota Vikings in Super Bowl IV.

And the Chiefs' second try turned out better than the first. Kansas City beat the Minnesota Vikings 23–7.

After Super Bowl IV, the AFL and NFL officially merged to become one league. The Chiefs would go on to have many thrilling moments after joining the NFL. But they are still waiting to match their glory days of the late 1960s.

CHAPTER 2

THE EARLY YEARS

Lamar Hunt dreamed of owning a pro football team. The son of a wealthy oilman, Hunt was in his twenties when he first tried to get an NFL franchise in Dallas, Texas. But every time he applied for a team, the league rejected him. These repeated rejections frustrated Hunt. In 1959, when he was 26 years old, Hunt tried something else.

Hunt approached other potential owners about founding their own professional football league. Seven months later, they had formed the AFL. Hunt was one of eight original owners.

The team owners met on August 14, 1959, at a hotel in Chicago. Hunt's team would play in his hometown and be called the Dallas Texans. The other seven teams would be

Lamar Hunt, right, shares a laugh with NFL commissioner Pete Rozelle before Super Bowl IV in January 1970.

the Boston Patriots, Buffalo Bills, Denver Broncos, Houston Oilers, Los Angeles Chargers, New York Titans, and a team based in Minneapolis, Minnesota. However, the Minneapolis owners dropped out before the first season because they were granted an NFL franchise. The Oakland Raiders replaced them as the AFL's eighth team.

Hunt's Dallas team was set to play its home games in the Cotton Bowl. Although they competed with the NFL's Dallas Cowboys, the Texans had decent local support. The team averaged 24,500 fans per game in its first season. That was the highest attendance in the league.

Part of the Texans' appeal was that they featured several former college stars from the state. Quarterback Cotton Davidson played at Baylor University in Waco. Fullback Jack Spikes was from Texas Christian University in Fort Worth. Running back Abner Haynes was from North Texas State, just outside of Dallas.

On September 10, 1960, the Texans opened AFL play by facing the Chargers in Los Angeles. Dallas jumped out to a 20–7 halftime lead, and an opening-day victory seemed to be in the works. But the second half did not go as planned for the Texans. They were held scoreless. Los Angeles ended up winning 21–20.

The Texans had much better luck the following week in Oakland. Davidson threw two touchdown passes. Spikes also kicked two field goals and ran for a touchdown. Dallas blasted the Raiders 34–16 for its first win.

The Texans had a powerful offense. They scored 30 or more points six times that season. But they fell short of the Western Division title. At 8–6, they finished the season two games behind the first-place Chargers. Haynes led the AFL with

LAMAR HUNT, FATHER OF THE AFL

Few people believed the AFL could survive. But after six seasons, the league was still growing. So much, in fact, that the NFL decided it was better to merge leagues than compete. The AFL and NFL champions began playing each other after the 1966 season. The two leagues combined to become one for the 1970 season. Hunt was a big reason for the AFL's success.

"Before there was a player, coach, or a general manager in the league, there was Lamar Hunt," former Boston Patriots owner William Sullivan said at Hunt's induction into the Pro Football Hall of Fame in 1972. "Hunt was the cornerstone, the integrity of the league. Without him, there would have been no AFL."

Texans running back Abner Haynes carries the ball against the Buffalo Bills in 1962.

875 rushing yards and nine touchdowns on the ground. His performance earned him player of the year honors in the AFL's first season.

The Texans took a step back in their second season, finishing 6–8. Their fall was fueled by a six-game losing streak during the middle of the season.

The 1962 season was a memorable one for the Texans and their fans. The team brought in Len Dawson. The quarterback had spent five seasons in the NFL but had started only two games. The Texans also signed Curtis McClinton, a rookie fullback who had a lot of potential.

The Texans plowed through the competition. They finished 11–3 and won the Western Division championship. Dawson took advantage of his opportunity to showcase his skills. He passed for more than 2,700 yards and an AFL-best 29 touchdowns that season. Dallas also had the league's highest-scoring offense. The dynamic backfield of Haynes and McClinton gave opponents headaches. Haynes ran for 1,049 yards and 13 touchdowns while McClinton added 604 rushing yards and two touchdowns.

Dallas faced its in-state rivals from Houston in the AFL Championship Game. The Oilers had won the AFL's first two titles and were heavily favored against the Texans on a windy and wet afternoon at Jeppesen Stadium in Houston. An energized crowd of 37,981 filled the stadium. A national television audience tuned in as well.

The Texans dominated the first half, charging out to a 17–0 lead behind two Haynes touchdowns.

MR. FRANCHISE

Between 1960 and 1962, Abner Haynes scored 44 touchdowns and tallied more than 4,000 yards of total offense. He was named the AFL's first rookie of the year and Most Valuable Player (MVP) in 1960. Texans head coach Hank Stram called Haynes a "franchise player."

"He was a franchise player before they talked about franchise players," Stram said. "He did it all— rushing, receiving, kickoff returns, punt returns."

But the defending champions tied the game at 17–17 in the fourth quarter. The Texans were on the brink of defeat with only three minutes left in the game.

Houston's George Blanda lined up to attempt a 42-yard field goal. But Texans linebacker Sherrill Headrick burst through the offensive line and got his hand on the ball to block the kick. The game headed to overtime.

A coin flip determined who got the ball first. The Texans won the coin toss. As team captain, Haynes was supposed to say they wanted to defend the side with the wind at their backs. Instead, Haynes said he wanted to kick with the wind. However, once he said the Texans wanted to kick, the officials cut him off and gave the Oilers their choice of ends to defend. Houston ended up receiving the kickoff and playing with the wind at its back.

"The players were excited and tugging at Abner," Texans coach Hank Stram said. "He just didn't understand the option. It was a mistake you don't like to make."

The mistake did not cost the Texans the game. Neither team scored during the first 15-minute overtime period. Then Dallas kicker Tommy Brooker made a game-winning 25-yard field goal

Curtis McClinton (32) and Len Dawson (16) pose with AFL commissioner Joe Foss after the Texans' 1962 AFL Championship win.

less than three minutes into the second overtime. Dallas won the game 20–17.

That AFL title would be the final highlight for the Texans. Despite their success, the team had trouble convincing fans they were at the same level as the NFL's Cowboys. Hunt decided to move the team to Kansas City before the 1963 season.

CHAPTER 3

GOING TO
KANSAS CITY

Lamar Hunt considered many cities when he decided to move his team. Atlanta, Miami, New Orleans, and Seattle were all options. But Hunt settled on Kansas City. His decision was sealed when the mayor agreed to expand Kansas City Municipal Stadium to 49,000 seats. The team changed its name to the Chiefs and entered the 1963 season with high hopes.

The 1963 AFL Draft had been a good one for the Chiefs. They acquired defensive tackle Buck Buchanan, guard Ed Budde, and linebacker Bobby Bell. The three played in a combined 527 career games with the Chiefs and earned 24 Pro Bowl selections. Buchanan and Bell were enshrined in the Pro Football Hall of Fame.

Guard Ed Budde lines up against the Vikings in Super Bowl IV.

Before the Chiefs officially took the field in Kansas City, however, tragedy struck the team. Stone Johnson, a running back with lots of potential, broke his neck in a preseason game. He died 10 days later.

The Chiefs opened their first season in Kansas City with a 59–7 win over the Denver Broncos. The victory was one of the few highlights during a difficult 5–7–2 season.

The 1964 season was not much better. With injuries to several key players, the Chiefs finished 7–7. An average of only 18,126 fans came to their home games. The other AFL owners became concerned about the Chiefs' future in Kansas City.

The Chiefs stayed in Kansas City. But their luck did not improve in 1965. They had drafted future Hall of Fame running back Gale Sayers from the University of Kansas. But they lost him in a bidding war with the NFL's Chicago Bears.

The team also experienced another tragedy. Running back Mack Lee Hill led the AFL in yards per carry in each of his first two seasons with the Chiefs. But Hill died while undergoing routine knee surgery that December. The cause of his death was a sudden and massive pulmonary embolism, a blockage in a lung artery.

On the field, Kansas City finished the year 7–5–2. But the luck of the Chiefs would change in 1966. Kansas City won its first three games on the road, including a 42–20 blowout of the defending AFL champion Buffalo Bills in Week 1. They returned home with a perfect 3–0 record and prepared for a rematch with the Bills.

A record crowd of 43,885 filled Municipal Stadium. And the fans had a lot to smile about early on. Dawson threw a 71-yard touchdown pass to Otis Taylor to give the Chiefs a 7–0 lead. The Chiefs led 14–6 after one quarter. But the Bills outscored the Chiefs 17–0 in the second half and left town with a 29–14 victory.

The loss did not rattle the confidence of the Chiefs, though. They went on to finish 11–2–1. They also won the Western Division by three games. The strong finish set up another showdown between

HALL OF FAME KICKER

Jan Stenerud was the first true placekicker to be inducted into the Pro Football Hall of Fame. He was inducted in 1992. The lanky Norwegian had come to the United States to attend Montana State on a skiing scholarship. He ended up excelling as a kicker, leading the league in field goals three times. He also made the Pro Bowl in 1984—at age 42—when he converted an NFL-best 87 percent of his field-goal tries (20 for 23) for the Minnesota Vikings. During his 19-year career, he made 373 field goals, which was an NFL record at the time of his retirement.

the Chiefs and Bills in the AFL Championship Game.

The Chiefs were confident heading into War Memorial Stadium in Buffalo. Dawson thrived on the cold and wet New Year's Day in western New York. He completed 16 of 24 passes for 227 yards and two touchdowns. The Chiefs won 31–7.

"This," Dawson said, "is the second most thrilling day of my life. The first most thrilling is coming up on January 15." That date might not have been as memorable as Dawson would have hoped. The Chiefs lost to the Packers in Super Bowl I.

The Chiefs had an uphill battle in the 1967 season trying to repeat as AFL champions. Kansas City finished 9–5 in an injury-filled season. But the team bounced back in 1968. The Chiefs finished 12–2 and tied the Oakland Raiders for first place in the Western Division. The tie set up a playoff game between the Chiefs and Raiders. However, Kansas City lost 41–6.

✗ Chiefs linebacker Willie Lanier returns an interception during the Super Bowl on January 11, 1970.

The 1969 AFL season was the last before the league merged with the NFL. The Chiefs overcame an injury to Dawson to finish 11–3. They were second in the Western Division to the Raiders, who finished 12–1–1. But because the AFL added another playoff round, the Chiefs were headed to the postseason.

First they faced quarterback Joe Namath and the New York Jets. Kansas City's stubborn defense gave the defending Super Bowl champions no breaks in a 13–6 victory.

Chiefs running back Warren McVea looks for space against the Houston Oilers in 1969.

The Chiefs then headed to Oakland to face the Raiders in the AFL Championship Game. Oakland had beaten Kansas City twice in the final four weeks of the season, but the two games were decided by a total of seven points. With the score tied 7–7 at halftime, Stram gave a motivational speech to his players. "'Turn it on,' I told them. 'Give it all you've got. It's in our grasp. Now squeeze it,'" Stram later recalled.

The defense continued to hold the Raiders in check, posting four interceptions on the day. Meanwhile, the offense put together two scoring drives in the second half to give the Chiefs a 17–7 victory. They were heading to Super Bowl IV.

There, the Chiefs met the NFL's Minnesota Vikings. The Chiefs players took pride in representing the AFL in Super Bowl IV. The players even wore "A-10" patches that symbolized the 10 years the AFL had been in existence. But the odds were against the Chiefs. The Vikings were known for their tough defense. They were favored to win by at least 12 points.

A record crowd of more than 80,000 fans showed up at Tulane Stadium in New Orleans for the game. The Chiefs went after the Vikings early. Running back Mike Garrett scored a touchdown and Jan Stenerud kicked three field goals. The Chiefs built a 16–0 halftime lead. Dawson played at his best, too. He completed 12 of his 17 passes. The highlight was a 46-yard touchdown pass to Taylor. That sealed a 23–7 victory.

The AFL era had ended on a high note, especially in Kansas City. The league had proved it was for real and was ready for the merger with the NFL. And the Chiefs were excited to show what they could do against their new foes.

CHAPTER 4

TOUGH TIMES

Kansas City was unable to build on the success of its Super Bowl win. The Chiefs missed the playoffs in 1970. They bounced back in 1971. Kicker Jan Stenerud nailed a field goal to give the Chiefs a late-season 16–14 win over the Raiders to clinch the West Division title.

The Chiefs faced the Miami Dolphins in the first round of the playoffs on Christmas Day. It was also the final game at Municipal Stadium in Kansas City. But it was not a happy exit for Chiefs fans. Stenerud missed a field-goal attempt with 35 seconds left in the fourth quarter. He had another game-winning try blocked in overtime. The Chiefs lost 27–24 in double overtime in the longest game in pro football history.

Chiefs owner Lamar Hunt poses in brand-new Arrowhead Stadium, which opened in 1972.

Kansas City was filled with excitement going into the 1972 season. That is because the Chiefs opened Arrowhead Stadium that year. It was considered the best stadium in the NFL at the time. Even legendary Chicago Bears owner George Halas was impressed. He called it "the most revolutionary, futuristic sports complex I have ever seen."

More than 79,000 fans turned out for the first regular-season game at the new stadium. The Chiefs opened their season with a rematch against the Dolphins. The players tried to keep their emotions in check before such a big game.

"We can't afford to get hyped up about this game with 13 to play afterward," Chiefs running back Ed Podolak said. "What happens if you get all emotionally involved and overpeaked and then lose?"

The Chiefs did lose the game, 20–10. They finished the year with

A TRUE HERO

Joe Delaney had a lot of potential as an NFL player. In college he was a two-time All-American. He was named the AFC Rookie of the Year in 1981 after rushing for more than 1,100 yards. But one day when he was back home in Louisiana in the summer of 1983, Delaney saw three children drowning in a hole filled with water. Even though he couldn't swim well, Delaney jumped in to try to save them. He did everything he could to rescue them. But two of three boys drowned, as did Delaney. To honor Delaney, no player has worn his No. 37 jersey since.

Chiefs linebacker Bobby Bell reacts to a play during a 1971 game. Bell was inducted into the Pro Football Hall of Fame in 1983.

an 8–6 record and missed the playoffs. Kansas City had another winning season in 1973 when it finished 7–5–2. But that was followed by several losing seasons.

The Chiefs' best players were getting old. The team spent most the 1970s with losing records and slowly seeing its best players retire. Kansas City tried to replace them with young talent. But it just didn't produce the same results.

The Chiefs went 8–8 in 1980. Then Kansas City won six of its first eight games in 1981. But the magic soon faded. The Chiefs finished 9–7 and didn't win more than eight games in a season between 1982 and 1985.

The team rebounded in 1986, however. With a 24–19 road win over the Pittsburgh Steelers in the season finale, the Chiefs qualified for the playoffs. But their luck ran out there. They lost 35–15 to the New York Jets in the first round.

After winning eight total games over the next two seasons, the Chiefs made another change. Marty Schottenheimer was hired as the new head coach. Schottenheimer had led the Cleveland Browns to a pair of American Football Conference (AFC) Championship Game appearances.

With Schottenheimer running the show, the Chiefs had new life. Linebacker Derrick Thomas was named the 1989 Defensive Rookie of the Year. Bruising running back Christian Okoye led the NFL in rushing. Behind the efforts of those two players, the Chiefs went 8–7–1, missing the playoffs by a half a game.

Thomas helped lead the Chiefs to success in 1990. Kansas City won six of its final seven games and made the playoffs. That was the start of six straight playoff seasons for the Chiefs. They lost to the Miami Dolphins in the first round, however. Kansas City also lost in the first round of the playoffs in 1991 and 1992. It was a time for another change.

So the Chiefs made a trade for Joe Montana. The star quarterback had led the San Francisco 49ers to four Super Bowl championships during the 1980s. The Chiefs also signed free agent Marcus Allen. He had been a star running back with the Los Angeles Raiders.

Montana and Allen made an immediate impact. The Chiefs finished 11–5. They took out the Steelers 27–24 in their playoff opener. Then they beat the Houston Oilers 28–20 for a berth in the AFC Championship Game. But that was the end of

MASTERFUL MARTY

Marty Schottenheimer already had a strong reputation when he was named head coach of the Chiefs in 1989. He found success right away in Kansas City, eventually winning three AFC West titles and waking the echoes of the team's early success in Kansas City. He averaged more than 10 wins per season in his 10 years with the Chiefs and retired in 2006 with 200 career NFL victories. Schottenheimer's biggest accomplishment, however, might have been his Chiefs going 18–3 against the rival Oakland Raiders.

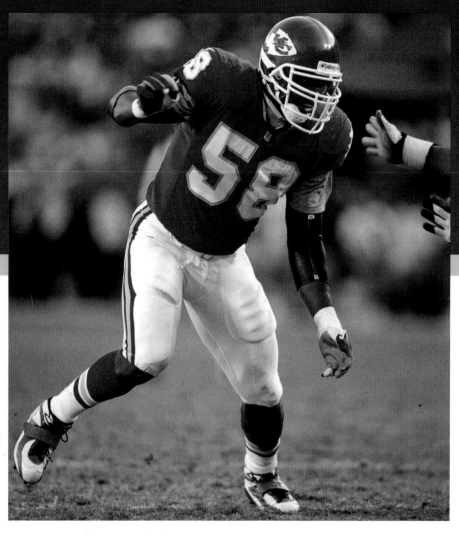

✕ Derrick Thomas was the NFL's defensive rookie of the year in 1989. He had 10 sacks and 75 tackles that season.

the line. Kansas City fell to the Buffalo Bills 30–13 in the AFC Championship Game.

The Chiefs beat the Raiders 19–9 on Christmas Eve to make the 1994 playoffs. Their run in the playoffs did not last long, however, as Kansas City fell to the Dolphins 27–17 in the first round. After that season, Montana retired from football.

In 1995 Chiefs fans had reason to believe their team might finally be good enough to return to the Super Bowl. Journeyman Steve Bono, Montana's backup in both San Francisco and Kansas City, earned his first chance as a starting quarterback at age 33. And he took full advantage of the opportunity, throwing 21 touchdown passes and just 10 interceptions on the season.

The Chiefs won 10 of their first 11 games and finished the regular season 13–3. They then hosted the Indianapolis Colts in a playoff game at frigid Arrowhead Stadium. But Chiefs fans were disappointed again. Bono threw three interceptions, and kicker Lin Elliott missed three field goals in the Chiefs' 10–7 loss. Nobody knew it at the time, but it was the end of an era for the Chiefs.

SACK MASTER

Derrick Thomas died from injuries suffered in an auto accident after the 1999 season. But he will go down as an all-time great in Kansas City. Thomas was a master at rushing the passer during the 1990s. He tallied 116.5 sacks during the decade. No other player in the NFL had more sacks in that time. He was enshrined in the Pro Football Hall of Fame in 2009.

CHAPTER 5

HITTING
THEIR STRIDE

The Chiefs' run of success was over for the time being. Kansas City made the postseason only once from 1996 to 2002, losing to the Denver Broncos in the 1997 playoffs. But an overhauled coaching staff and roster soon built a record-setting offense that could win games, too.

Kansas City hired head coach Dick Vermeil before the 2001 season. Vermeil had guided the St. Louis Rams to the Super Bowl title just two years earlier. One of his first moves in Kansas City was trading for quarterback Trent Green. The two had worked together in St. Louis. The Chiefs also added running back Priest Holmes before the season.

Holmes had been undrafted out of college and was primarily a backup with the Baltimore Ravens. But with the

Running back Priest Holmes shattered NFL records when he joined the Chiefs in 2001.

Chiefs, he exploded. In 2003 he set a new NFL record with 27 touchdowns. The Chiefs were on fire, too. Behind an explosive offense, they started the season with nine straight wins. That was a team record.

At the end of the regular season, the Chiefs were 13–3 and the second seed in the AFC. They hosted the Indianapolis Colts in the playoffs. Both teams were known for their explosive offenses. Neither offense had to punt in the game. But the Chiefs came out on the wrong end again. Indianapolis won 38–31.

The Chiefs missed the playoffs the next two years despite some amazing individual performances. In 2004 tight end Tony Gonzalez caught 102 passes to lead the NFL. And in 2005, running back Larry Johnson rushed for a team-record 1,750 yards and added 20 touchdowns.

PRIEST HOLMES

After serving as a backup for most of his four years with the Baltimore Ravens, Priest Holmes got a chance in Kansas City to become a starting running back in 2001. He didn't waste that opportunity. Holmes rushed for 1,555 yards in his first season with the Chiefs to become the first undrafted player to lead the NFL in rushing since Joe Perry in 1954. He was one of the league's top running backs in his first three seasons with the Chiefs. However, injuries began to pile up, and he played in only 19 games over the next four seasons before retiring at age 34.

✗ Tight end Tony Gonzalez went to 10 straight Pro Bowls during his 12-year career with the Chiefs.

Vermeil resigned after the 2005 season, and the Chiefs briefly showed some signs of improvement under coach Herm Edwards. They reached the playoffs in his first season, thanks

✗ Andy Reid helped turn the Chiefs offense into a nightmare for opposing defenses.

in large part to another monster year from Johnson, who broke his own team record with 1,789 rushing yards and added 17 more touchdowns. But they again lost to the Colts in the playoffs, this time 23–8.

The Chiefs went through ups and downs over the next decade in the search for playoff success. The tide began to turn when the Chiefs brought in Andy Reid as their new head coach. With the Philadelphia Eagles Reid was known for his innovative offenses, and he quickly built Kansas City into a playoff team.

Reid traded for quarterback Alex Smith in 2013 to run the offense. The Chiefs made the playoffs five times in Reid's first six seasons as head coach. In January 2016 they defeated the Houston Texans in an AFC Wild Card game for their first playoff victory in more than 20 years. In 2017 the Chiefs won their second straight AFC West title. It was the first time ever that Kansas City had won back-to-back division titles.

The next year was even better. Prior to the 2018 season, the Chiefs shook up their roster by trading Smith to Washington. That put the team in the hands of second-year quarterback Patrick Mahomes. Even though Mahomes had seen

TONY GONZALEZ

Tony Gonzalez played basketball and football at the University of California, but he chose to pursue a career in the NFL. That was fortunate for the Chiefs, who selected Gonzalez in the first round of the 1997 NFL Draft. The durable tight end missed only two games in 12 seasons in Kansas City. Gonzalez was named to 10 Pro Bowls and was a first-team All-Pro pick six times. He spent five more productive seasons in Atlanta before retiring in 2013 with career totals that are unlikely to be matched by any other tight end.

action in just one game as a rookie, Reid had faith in the team's 2017 first-round draft pick. And Mahomes rewarded that faith with a spectacular season. He opened the year by winning the AFC Offensive Player of the Week honors in each of the first two weeks of the season. And he broke Peyton Manning's NFL record by throwing 13 touchdown passes in the first three games of the year. He went on to become the second quarterback in NFL history with 5,000 passing yards and 50 touchdown passes in the same season and was a shoo-in for the NFL MVP Award.

The Chiefs started the year with nine wins in their first 10 games before dropping a 54–51 shootout against the Rams in Los Angeles. They recovered to go 12–4 and earn home-field advantage throughout the AFC playoffs. A 31–13 win over the Colts put them in the AFC Championship Game against Tom Brady and the New England Patriots at chilly Arrowhead Stadium. The Chiefs trailed 14–0 at halftime before rallying to take the lead in the fourth quarter. However, the game went to overtime and the Patriots scored a touchdown on their opening drive to win it, ending the Chiefs' dream season.

Mahomes's play got fans talking about a return to the glory days of the 1960s in Kansas City. Support from wide receiver Tyreek Hill, tight end Travis Kelce, and a strong running game

✗ Patrick Mahomes took the NFL by storm after securing the Chiefs' starting quarterback job in 2018.

gave the Chiefs one of the top offenses in the NFL. Chiefs fans hope it's just a matter of time before they're back in the Super Bowl.

TIMELINE

After failing to be granted an NFL franchise, Lamar Hunt helps found the rival AFL.

✖ 1959

The Dallas Texans play their first season in the AFL and finish 8–6.

✖ 1960

Dallas wins the West Division championship and defeats the Houston Oilers in the AFL Championship Game.

✖ 1962

Unable to compete with the NFL's Dallas Cowboys for fans, the Texans move to Missouri and become the Kansas City Chiefs.

✖ 1963

Kansas City wins the AFL title and plays the Green Bay Packers in Super Bowl I on January 15. The Chiefs lose 35–10.

✖ 1967

Kansas City wins the final AFL Championship Game and faces the Minnesota Vikings in Super Bowl IV on January 11. The Chiefs win 23–7.

✖ 1970

The Chiefs lose to the Dolphins 27–24 in double overtime on December 25 in their final game at Municipal Stadium.

✖ 1971

The Chiefs play their first season at Arrowhead Stadium. They fail to make the playoffs, however, finishing 8–6.

✖ 1972

Head coach Hank Stram and the Chiefs part ways after a 5–9 season.

✖ 1974

Kansas City finishes the year 9–7 for its first winning season since 1973.

✖ 1981

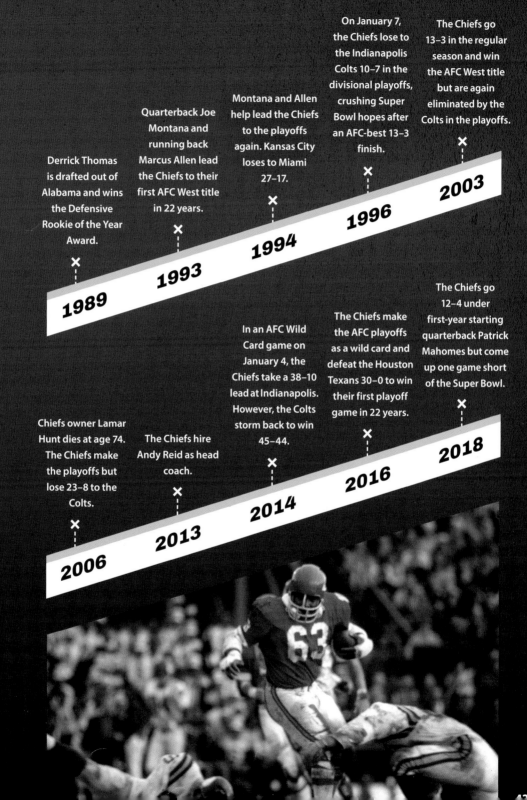

Derrick Thomas is drafted out of Alabama and wins the Defensive Rookie of the Year Award.

✕

1989

Quarterback Joe Montana and running back Marcus Allen lead the Chiefs to their first AFC West title in 22 years.

✕

1993

Montana and Allen help lead the Chiefs to the playoffs again. Kansas City loses to Miami 27–17.

✕

1994

On January 7, the Chiefs lose to the Indianapolis Colts 10–7 in the divisional playoffs, crushing Super Bowl hopes after an AFC-best 13–3 finish.

✕

1996

The Chiefs go 13–3 in the regular season and win the AFC West title but are again eliminated by the Colts in the playoffs.

✕

2003

Chiefs owner Lamar Hunt dies at age 74. The Chiefs make the playoffs but lose 23–8 to the Colts.

✕

2006

The Chiefs hire Andy Reid as head coach.

✕

2013

In an AFC Wild Card game on January 4, the Chiefs take a 38–10 lead at Indianapolis. However, the Colts storm back to win 45–44.

✕

2014

The Chiefs make the AFC playoffs as a wild card and defeat the Houston Texans 30–0 to win their first playoff game in 22 years.

✕

2016

The Chiefs go 12–4 under first-year starting quarterback Patrick Mahomes but come up one game short of the Super Bowl.

✕

2018

QUICK STATS

FRANCHISE HISTORY

Dallas Texans, 1960–62 (AFL)
Kansas City Chiefs, 1963–70 (AFL)
1970– (NFL)

SUPER BOWLS
(wins in bold)

1966 (I), **1969 (IV)**

AFL CHAMPIONSHIP GAMES (1960–69, *wins in bold*)

1962, 1966, **1969**

DIVISION CHAMPIONSHIPS (SINCE 1970 AFL-NFL MERGER)

1971, 1993, 1995, 1997, 2003, 2010, 2016, 2017

KEY COACHES

Andy Reid (2013–): 65–31,
  2–5 (playoffs)
Marty Schottenheimer (1989–98):
  101–58–1, 3–7 (playoffs)
Hank Stram (1960–74): 124–76–10,
  5–3 (playoffs)

KEY PLAYERS *(position, seasons with team)*

Bobby Bell (DE-LB, 1963–74)
Buck Buchanan (DT, 1963–75)
Ed Budde (G, 1963–76)
Len Dawson (QB, 1962–75)
Tony Gonzalez (TE, 1997–2008)
Abner Haynes (HB, 1960–64)
Priest Holmes (RB, 2001–07)
Derrick Johnson (LB, 2005–17)
Willie Lanier (LB, 1967–77)
Ed Podolak (RB, 1969–77)
Johnny Robinson (DB, 1960–71)
Will Shields (G, 1993–06)
Gary Spani (LB, 1978–86)
Jan Stenerud (K, 1967–79)
Art Still (DE, 1978–87)
Otis Taylor (WR, 1965–75)
Derrick Thomas (LB, 1989–99)
Emmitt Thomas (CB, 1966–78)
Jim Tyrer (T, 1961–73)

HOME FIELDS

Arrowhead Stadium (1972–)
Kansas City Municipal Stadium
  (1963–71)
Cotton Bowl (1960–62)

* All statistics through 2018 season

QUOTES AND ANECDOTES

Many people believed the AFL was a bad idea. As such, they nicknamed the eight founding owners in the league the "Foolish Club." Dallas Texans owner Lamar Hunt was among those owners. The league played a 14-game schedule. Every team played the others twice. It turned out to be a good thing for fans. They were given an opportunity to see every team in the league each year.

"It was really tough because there is no question that I had a lot to do with losing the game. It was hard to take, but time, I guess, heals everything. The only thing I can do is try to block out the memory of what happened."
—Jan Stenerud about his poor performance in the 1971 playoff loss to Miami

Kansas City's Dante Hall tied an NFL record with his sixth career kickoff return for a touchdown in an October 2005 game against the Philadelphia Eagles. He also returned six punts for touchdowns in his career. In 2003 Hall returned kicks for touchdowns in four straight games.

Former Kansas City running back Christian Okoye once punished defenses with his hard running ability. He went on to help young boys and girls through his foundation. He enjoys being a role model. "Anytime a person succeeds, whether you like it or not, you are a role model," Okoye said. "Whether I like it or not, it is the case. I like it. I chose to embrace it."

The Chiefs have a passionate group of fans. They pack into Arrowhead Stadium and can make a lot of noise. In 2014 the fans set a world record for loudest crowd roar at a stadium. The noise was 142.2 decibels. Kansas City celebrated the world record and a 41–14 win over the New England Patriots.

GLOSSARY

attendance
The number of fans at a game or the total number of fans attending games in a season.

blitz
When a linebacker or defensive back attacks the line of scrimmage to stop a run or sack the quarterback.

clinch
To officially settle something, such as a berth in the playoffs.

draft
A system that allows teams to acquire new players coming into a league.

franchise player
An athlete who is not simply the best player on their team, but one a team builds around for the foreseeable future.

legendary
A player who is generally regarded as one of the best to ever play.

merge
Join with another to create something new, such as a company, a team, or a league.

retire
To end one's career.

rival
An opponent with whom a player or team has a fierce and ongoing competition.

rookie
A professional athlete in his or her first year of competition.

ticket broker
A person who purchases tickets to an event and then resells them.

MORE INFORMATION

BOOKS

Cohn, Nate. *Kansas City Chiefs*. New York: AV2 by Weigl, 2018.

Howell, Brian. *NFL's Top Ten Games*. Minneapolis, MN: Abdo Publishing, 2017.

Kortemeier, Todd. *Kansas City Chiefs*. Minneapolis, MN: Abdo Publishing, 2017.

ONLINE RESOURCES

To learn more about the Kansas City Chiefs, visit **abdobooklinks.com** or scan this QR code. These links are routinely monitored and updated to provide the most current information available.

PLACES TO VISIT

Arrowhead Stadium
One Arrowhead Dr.
Kansas City, MO 64129
816–920–9400
chiefs.com/stadium

This has been the Kansas City Chiefs' home stadium since 1972.

Pro Football Hall of Fame
2121 George Halas Dr., NW
Canton, OH 44708
330–456–8207
profootballhof.com

This hall of fame and museum highlights the greatest players and moments in the history of the AFL and the NFL. Those enshrined who are affiliated with the Chiefs include Len Dawson, Lamar Hunt, and Derrick Thomas.

INDEX

ABOUT THE AUTHOR

Tony Hunter is a writer from Castle Rock, Colorado. This is his first children's book series. He lives with his daughter and his trusty Rottweiler, Dan.